D1505264

The Inner Beauty Series
Defining Your Worth in the Eyes of God

UNDERSTAND *Your True* MEASURE

Lisa Bevere

UNDERSTAND YOUR TRUE MEASURE by Lisa Bevere
Published by Charisma House
A part of Strang Communications Company
600 Rinehart Road
Lake Mary, Florida 32746
www.charismahouse.com

Unless otherwise noted, all Scripture quotations are from the Holy Bible, New International Version. Copyright © 1973, 1978, 1984, International Bible Society. Used by permission.

Scripture quotations marked NKJV are from the New King James Version of the Bible. Copyright © 1979, 1980, 1982 by Thomas Nelson, Inc., publishers. Used by permission.

Cover design by Rachel Campbell

Library of Congress Catalog Card Number: 2001099919
International Standard Book Number: 0-88419-839-1

02 03 04 05 87654321
Printed in the United States of America

Contents

Introduction

his first book of the Inner Beauty Series is my heart. If you have ever felt as if you just do not fit in, this book is for you. It's for you if you have felt that you are on the outside looking in, wishing there was more than what you've seen. This is not merely a book about women's issues— it's about *heart issues.* God is calling us to be more than we've ever been—more than we have ever envisioned that we could become.

At the very onset of this book, I want to challenge you to read it differently than you read other books. I want you to *participate* with this book, not just read it in quiet thought. I want you to dare to address the issues raised within these pages on a very real and tangible level. I want the truths in this book to become woven into the fabric of your life. The only way for this to happen is for you to apply these truths personally.

This is easier said than done. It is always easier to remove yourself emotionally from a book and just process its contents mentally while remaining very detached. But this is not where change is forged. It is the truth we *live,* not the truth we *know,* that sets us free. In order to find such truth, we must *be honest* with ourselves, *answer* some questions and then *change* the way we have looked at things.

The degree to which you are honest, open and transparent is the degree to which you will allow the light of God's Word to penetrate. Only God's Word can separate the precious from the vile.

To accomplish this, I invite you to keep a journal or notepad handy as you read. There will be questions only you can answer, and it is important that you record these answers as you go. These questions may also bring to light questions of your own, ones that you will want to write down so you can bring them before the Father later during times of prayer.

Make the establishment of God's truth a priority in your life. The truth you uncover in the five books that are a part of the Inner Beauty Series will prepare you to live your life radiating the inner beauty of your heart—the true radiance of the woman of God you were meant to be.

—LISA BEVERE

Adapted from Lisa Bevere, *The True Measure of a Woman,* xii–xiii.

INNER BEAUTY TIP

GOD AWAKENS AN
INQUISITIVE QUESTIONING IN US
WHEN HE WANTS US
TO GO SEARCHING
FOR ANSWERS.

Asking
Questions

I praise you because I am fearfully and
wonderfully made.

—Psalm 139:14

his book is the culmination of my ongoing
search for answers to a series of questions
with which I have wrestled since my teen
years. They are questions I believe every woman—
no matter her walk in life or experience—mulls
over as the different seasons of her life ebb and
flow. These are simple questions really—questions
like, "How do I fit in or relate to the world around
me?" and "What is the measure of my worth?"

While I believed I knew the answers to such

questions, not too long ago I had the opportunity to view them in a new and different light. It was an unexpected moment when I knew my outlook would be altered permanently.

I had escaped the noise and clamor of a house filled with four young sons to enjoy the quiet of my husband's office after hours. It was the place I had chosen to conduct a radio interview for my book *Out of Control and Loving It!* Although its title conveyed an image of high energy and lots of activity, I knew the radio listeners would still appreciate a quiet background while I discussed the book. Radio is wonderful and relaxed because no one can see you. So, clad in baseball cap and a warm-up suit, I waited for my interviewer to call, since the program would be taped via phone to air later.

A few weeks earlier I had spoken with Sarah, my interviewer, to schedule the show and get acquainted. She was pleasant and professional. She was honest and let me know that she had yet to read my book, and that she would probably only have time to scan it before we spoke again. Sarah explained that she received so many books to review that she rarely read them all the way through prior to interviewing the authors. She suggested that I come up with some questions and arrive at some idea of what I wanted to discuss. She said she would call a few minutes early so we could go over my questions before the interview.

So there I was, in the stillness of my husband's empty office, flipping through my book and making notes for myself in the margins as I folded down the corners of pages containing points of interest. As I did this, I prayed that those who needed to hear this interview would be drawn to listen and, most of all, that it would glorify God. I waited, a little nervous, never suspecting the impact the interview would have on me.

The phone broke the silence and startled me. It was Sarah, but this time she sounded excited. "I don't want to talk now and diminish your answers on the air, but I have *read* your book! And we need to address some things. I have my questions ready. I want to highlight your *gossip chapter* in our interview!"

The gossip chapter! I hadn't marked anything from that chapter! Sarah's enthusiasm had caught me totally off guard. I had planned to talk about the anger chapter. Frantically I flipped pages, dog-earring some of them and hastily attaching sticky notes. I took a deep breath and reminded myself of the question my husband always poses whenever he sees me spinning off into such flurries of panic just before an interview: "Didn't *you* write the book?" The truth was *I had,* and the gossip chapter was especially personal!

For the next hour Sarah and I discussed the tendency of women to gossip and the various ulterior motives behind it—namely...fear. Sarah had blown asunder any facade of professionalism when she opened the program with a candid and broken confession of her own tendency to gossip. She pleaded with the unseen radio audience to be open and transformed in this area of their own personal lives. She confessed how, in her profession, she had always considered gossip to be "networking."

The questions Sarah asked probed deeper than those of an unbiased interviewer. They echoed the cries and excitement of a searching heart that had suddenly found truth. Together we shared, pleaded and prayed with our audience. When the interview was over, we continued to talk. Sarah opened up even more with me, and we ended by praying together. As I hung up the phone, I felt as though I had just said good-bye to a college roommate. For a moment I sat alone, acutely aware that something different had transpired.

HEARING HEART TO HEART

Although I had never seen her, I felt I knew this woman more intimately than most of the women I meet in person. I did not know whether she was young or old, rich or poor, fat or thin, black or white, blonde, brunette or redhead. There had been no way to read her facial expressions and body language as we talked. I couldn't take note of whether she was dressed for success or dressed for comfort. Yet I felt I knew her.

Then it dawned on me that this bond might not have been made if we had met in person. We may have done that unconscious checkout of each other, and we may have been influenced by each other's visual impressions. Though I could never pick her out of a crowd, I felt I knew this woman called Sarah more than some of my own neighbors. I had not *seen* her, but I had *heard* her—not the fake her, the *real* her. I had heard something I could never look upon, because I had heard her heart.

Seizing the moment, the Holy Spirit arrested my racing thoughts and said, *"That is how I know you."* He whispered, "I cannot see you, for you are hidden in Christ. I can only hear you. It is your spoken words and the unbroken communication of your heart to which I listen."

That was right! Because I had no righteousness of my own, the righteousness of Jesus had been appropriated to me in redemption. God could not look upon me, so I was covered in the sin offering of Jesus the Christ. Not unlike a radio interview, it didn't matter to the Holy Spirit what I looked like; it only mattered what I said. Of course, the Holy Spirit had another frequency—one that even the strongest satellite could not monitor. It was the frequency of the silent communication of my heart!

That's good—and that's bad! Good, because unlike us, God neither judges nor is affected by what He sees. Bad, because I tend to be more aware of what I see than what I do not see. This means I often unconsciously measure myself by parameters God does not even use! It's bad, because though I had really grown in certain spiritual dimensions—my confession, for instance—I still had not conquered the vivid and violent battleground of my thoughts.

> The Holy Spirit had another frequency—the frequency of the silent communication of my heart!

That night my husband and I went out on a much-needed dinner date. Over our meal I shared with him what had happened during the radio interview that afternoon. I explained to John how women tend to look at things. I used different scenarios to illustrate the tendency toward competition and the measuring of each other by what we see or perceive. I confessed my tendency to do this and explained how frustrated I was when I knew I was being reduced to what I looked like or wore. Surely I was not alone in my frustration. My spirit sensed such an urgency for truth. I was tired of hearing the pat excuses I had always so readily accepted: "You know women; that is just the way they are!" or, "It's a woman thing!" Such statements may sound true, but they are not the truth!

I wanted God's truth, not excuses, not even for myself. This would mean peeling away some layers, like the dry and dirty outer skin of an onion— layer after layer of misconceptions and bad information until I found some pure truth.

QUESTIONS AND ANSWERS

God awakens an inquisitive questioning in us when He wants us to go searching for answers. To learn, we must first ask questions. Questions are not always comfortable. Remember school, when you had a question, and you were afraid you would sound stupid if you asked it? Or when the teacher asked you a question, and you were unsure of the answer?

Well, here is our question, the one we will repeatedly ask: *What is the true measure of a woman?*

You could poll any mixed group of people and receive a variety of answers. Each answer would be spawned by variances in culture, gender and age. Ask a preschooler, and the standard of a woman is bound to be that child's mother. To an older child, the measure would broaden to include teachers, athletes or performers. To a young adult or teenager, a woman is measured in comparison with the images projected by models, Hollywood personalities and the cultural influences of their age group. Things like how a woman looks. What she wears. By this time, the physical and sexual differences are pronounced and overshadow the innocence of a child's former perceptions of a woman.

I wanted God's truth, not excuses, not even for myself.

If we are more selective and question only a certain group of women, we'll receive yet another sampling of answers. Personal and vulnerable answers, the ones you only get when men are not around.

But I don't believe we will find the answer we

are searching for in any of these public polls or personal opinions. Nor can it be drawn from my experiences or those of others—these are too limited. Our culture cannot answer us. It is tormented with too many questions of its own, questions it cannot answer because of inconsistency and the prevalent influence of the spirit of this world. We could ask our mothers, but like us, most of them are still searching.

The written word has the power to probe directly into the secret place of your silent thoughts.

QUESTIONS

Although I am not conducting an official opinion poll, I am going to question you—even knowing that I may never hear your answer. The written word has the power to probe directly into the secret place of your silent thoughts. You cannot hear my voice, and I cannot hear your answer. Through the pages of this book, you and I can communicate on a more intimate, unspoken level, one that would not be possible even if we were face to face.

You may have already toyed with what your reply will be. Now I will ask you directly, and I want you to stop and write your answer down in the space provided.

What is the true measure of a woman?

_____

_____

You may be thinking, *Hey, if I had the answer, I wouldn't be reading this book!* Please remember what we covered in the introduction. (If you didn't read it, please go back.) This is a participation—not an observation—book. To learn, we must not merely see but truly understand what we already know. It is imperative that you and I interact, although at this point you may find this awkward or difficult. You may find this question hard to answer specifically. That's all right; be vague. And if you have no idea, write down, "I have no idea!" Above all, be honest. This is not a test, and your answer will not be graded. No one will even see your answer unless you choose to show them. This book is simply a search for truth.

I don't presume to know all life's answers, but this book is from my heart to yours, and I believe it bears a glimpse of our Father's heart, too. Through its quiet pages, we will talk—and it is my prayer that the power of the Holy Spirit will overshadow all we discuss so that together we may glean His wisdom.

I challenge you to join me in this search to understand your true measure. You must already be curious. As you turn these pages and read the truth of God, it will remove the scales that kept you from seeing. Let His light illuminate your eyes.

Pray with me:

> *Father God, reveal Your truth to me by Your Word and Spirit. Lord, give me eyes to see, ears to hear and a heart that perceives and understands. Above all these, Lord, grant me a willing and pliable heart that will believe and apply Your truth so*

that it may bring forth Your beauty in my life. I give You permission to change my perspective. Reveal Yourself, for You are the way, the truth and the life. Amen.

Believe that He will.

Adapted from *The True Measure of a Woman*, 1–7.

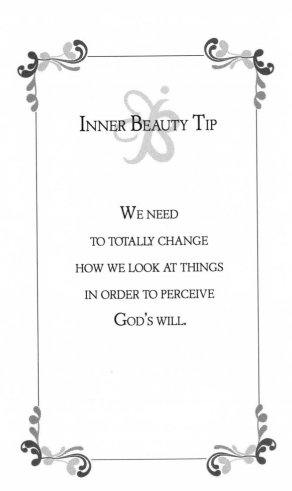

INNER BEAUTY TIP

WE NEED

TO TOTALLY CHANGE

HOW WE LOOK AT THINGS

IN ORDER TO PERCEIVE

GOD'S WILL.

2

Cleaning Closets

Do not conform any longer to the pattern of this world, but be transformed by the renewing of your mind. Then you will be able to test and approve what God's will is—his good, pleasing and perfect will.

—ROMANS 12:2

Our search for truth could be compared to cleaning out a bedroom closet. I usually tackle cleaning out my closet only when I absolutely have to. It is only when I find clutter and disorder so intimidating that I can stand it no longer that I finally resolve to clean my closet. A variety of circumstances will inspire my rampage to clean and organize. It may be that I see someone in need of something that I know hangs unused in my closet. Or perhaps a move will necessitate such a cleaning jag. My need to clean may simply arise in retaliation after innocently walking in to pull a sweater off the shelf—and the whole stack leaps out, toppling sweaters onto my head and then onto the floor. Now a challenge has gone forth to clean out that closet—or else, and I pick up the gauntlet, determined to set all things in order.

I counterattack, grabbing fallen clothes and everything else from the shelves and hanging rods. These items are rapidly transported into the light and tumbled onto the master bed, with the overflow portioned to the living-room sofa. With everything out, I vacuum the closet floor and pick up the stray dry cleaning tags, safety pins and pocket change as I work. Now my closet seems much bigger and far less intimidating. I'm ready to reorganize and rehang. I go over each item before hanging it up or granting it shelf space. I ask an assortment of questions. *Do I still need this maternity dress if I'm not planning any more children?* My mind argues, *That's what you thought two children ago!* But I fight back, *No! I'll give it away.*

Then I make some observations. "Oh no, *this*

was hung up dirty!"..."I stained this the first time I wore it"..."I paid too much to just throw it away"..."Maybe a new cleaning product will come out that removes three-year-old stains." Finally, I conclude, "No! Lisa, just *throw it away!*"

I find there is just no room for that heavy winter outfit in my July closet. So I put it in off-season storage. After discarding the prolific hangers that seem to have multiplied since my last closet purge, I discover there is space to hang more clothes when all the empty coat hangers are cleared out. With all the unnecessary and inappropriate items removed, I now have room for the important things—the things I can use.

This whole process has provided a moment of truth for me. I can often gauge my spiritual well-being by seeing what I fight to hang on to.

TACKLING THE TOUGH ISSUES

In this chapter, we are going to tackle the closets of our minds. It is so much easier when you don't have to face it alone. I'm going to help you with this process. I will face it *with you*. There are many outfits (past experiences) and accessories (thought

17

processes) that you should never wear again. They are dated, they no longer fit and they rob space from what you should be wearing right now. Some items should be thrown away. Others should be given to those who could really use them.

> Pass on the faithfulness
> of God and His provision
> in your life, and share it
> with others.

Go ahead...examine the contents of your closet. Is that item from long ago, one you kept for safety—just in case it came back in style? Was it trendy then but now out of date? (Remember, fashion and events never repeat themselves in quite the same way—so pitch it!) Has it outlived its usefulness to you but could be passed on to bless another? (Passing things on to the next generation keeps them fresh and alive; retaining them means they get musty and old.)

Pass on the faithfulness of God and His provision

in your life, and share it with others. As we share these "outfits" of our testimony with others, we help those who are yet struggling with areas we have since overcome. Sharing in this manner renews our own faith, because we are encouraged to believe that God will be faithful once again.

Some items are soiled with guilt and must be washed in the Word of God before they can be worn again. Others bear stains that can't be removed. Don't mourn their loss—just throw them away. They represent the various disappointments and failures in the past, things we need to forgive and forget. In this closet we will find things we thought were lost. We'll come to the realization that some items cannot be found in the confines of our closet.

Cleaning closets is comparable to the process of renewing our minds.

> Do not conform any longer to the pattern of this world, but be transformed by the renewing of your mind. Then you will be able to test and approve what God's will is—his good, pleasing and perfect will.
>
> —ROMANS 12:2

We want to weigh out, agree with and apply God's truth in our lives. This requires nothing short of a transformation in our minds. We need to change totally how we look at things in order to perceive God's will. We cannot determine His plan through the clutter of the counsel of man and the plans of this world. We may rest assured of three characteristics of God's plan for us:

1. It is for good.
2. It is pleasing to Him.
3. It is perfect.

And it is never inappropriate, although at first it may seem uncomfortable. God is ultimately more concerned with our *condition* than our *comfort*. This means there will be times of temporary discomfort in order to bring about eternal comfort. What He provides is drawn from timeless wisdom and always in good taste. It is flawless and void of stains, rips and imperfections. God wants to outfit our mind with a whole new outlook.

Just like our closets, our minds can become cluttered by the patterns or trends of this world. These outfits, or thought processes, may look as if they belong in our closets the first few years they take up residence. But with the passage of time, they soon appear threadbare and out of sorts. They fit too tight or too loose, too long or too short. Unless our closets—minds—are cleared out and reorganized on a timely and regular basis, we will not be able to test and apply God's truth to our lives.

The standard for determining what remains in our minds and on the rack always must be God's Word. Since the objective of this book is to locate and apply truth, as unpleasant as it may initially be, we are going to need to clean some closets. Left to themselves, our minds will accumulate clutter. And clutter needs to be stored, refreshed or removed. If we don't clear out the clutter, we will lack the necessary space for the wisdom and fresh insights that God longs to provide for us.

AS LITTLE CHILDREN

Often when I pick up my children from school they will tumble into the car and excitedly share some new tidbit of knowledge they have gleaned that day. It begins with a challenge, "Mom, did you know…?" Often I will already have this knowledge stored somewhere in the deep recesses of my memory, but in response to my children's excitement—and because I want to hear their unique perspectives—I'll answer, "Tell me!" Then their high-pitched voices will take on a lower, slower, more serious, almost scholarly tone as they explain from their new and fresh view a science, math or history fact.

Their zeal usually reawakens my awareness of this information, along with the memory of when I learned such facts. When the boys finish their discourse, they almost always conclude with their original question: "Did you know that, Mom?"

The standard for determining what remains in our minds and on the rack always must be God's Word.

I'll answer truthfully, "I did—but I had forgotten that I knew it, because I haven't used that information for so long." My answer always puzzles them. At their age, almost everything they learn is still actively retained because they apply their present knowledge to gather more. Consequently, their mental "closets" are revolving storehouses of actively used "clothes."

Jesus admonishes us to approach the kingdom of God as little children. (See Matthew 18:3.)

This is not a call to immature or childish behavior, but to become childlike. One such childlike attribute is to be inquisitive. My children sometimes exhaust me with their many questions, but a child who does not ask questions is a child who has stopped learning. And a child who is not questioned will not be accurately positioned for learning. That is why children are tested at school each year. It is to see if they can apply what they have mastered.

When my children transferred schools, they were tested for placement to confirm that they had been equipped with the tools necessary to learn in their new environment. When we are childlike, we will maintain an attitude that is forever teachable.

God has created us to respond to our surroundings with excitement, awe and wonder. This wonder will inspire us to ask questions. I loved watching the joy of learning light up the eyes of my children when, as young children, they discovered something new or mastered some new skill. If I just lifted them high enough to touch a leaf, they were thrilled and stretched their arms higher yet to embrace the entire branch. To a young child, every discovery is an adventure, a new tool he can use in his pursuit of understanding the world around him.

As adults, we are to approach life in the same childlike manner. But often our mental closets are too cluttered with outdated information and the cynical outlook of this world. Without our full realization, this clutter colors our perception of everything. To make way for the new, we must rid ourselves of the old—the way we previously looked at things, the standards we have used to measure ourselves in the past, the scale by which we measure others, the limits fear has placed on our lives, the wasteland of our past that has to be left behind. We will address these various forms of clutter individually and in depth. After all, as a woman I know where you are—though I may not know exactly where you have been.

"WHY ME, LORD?"

I am right where you are. As a woman, wife and mother of four boys, I face the same pressures you face. They are often magnified by a husband who travels at least weekly, my editing and writing deadlines and assorted office responsibilities. Add to all this that I also travel and speak.

I have often questioned God's wisdom of choosing me when I already feel totally incapable. One such question-and-answer session happened while I showered (one of the few places I can think undisturbed) in preparation before speaking to a large group of women. I had brought my youngest son, who was still nursing, and had not slept well in the strange hotel room, where he tossed around all night. At that moment he was at my feet playing in the shower so I could keep an eye on him.

Looking down at him, I asked myself, *What am I doing here? I have already spoken to these women four times over the last three years. I feel as though I have nothing left to say. God, You should get someone professional to do this—not a breast-feeding mother of four!*

I was venting and did not even expect an answer. But nevertheless, an answer came while I wrestled the tangle of the billowing shower curtain away from my slippery son.

"You are right where they are! Therefore, you will not talk down to them. You'll have compassion on them. Be real and transparent, and they will see Me in you."

At that point, I could not even see myself through the steam on the bathroom mirror. I was doubtful, but I felt a peace settle over me.

Later that morning as I entered the crowded sanctuary, I felt the anointing presence of God come upon me. It was very real and tangible, as though someone had come up behind me and draped a cloak about me. It comforted me. My mind again was full of questions as I walked to the platform: *What am I doing here?* My heart knew the answer.

FAR FROM PERFECT

I have attended many women's meetings. Sometimes I knew I was in trouble as soon as the speaker walked up to the pulpit. From what was said and the image projected by the speakers, I got the impression that their lives were perfect, their children were perfect, their marriages were perfect and their finances were blessed and abundant.

In comparison, I felt like a failure. Although I *wanted* to be like them, I feared I was too different …too imperfect.

I would listen intently to their perfect messages, taking extensive notes. Yet, while my head mentally identified with the principles they taught, my heart did not. I would leave some of these meetings with a list of advice that didn't seem at all applicable to where I was. Their solutions of taking bubble baths and making more time for myself did not fit in with my busy lifestyle. I left other meetings feeling defeated. If only I read my Bible more often and pray three hours a day, everything would be perfect! For whatever reason, their words seemed only to increase the already heavy yoke I bore. I was simultaneously impressed by these women and intimidated by them.

Over the years I have had one opportunity after another to find out that the lives represented by these speakers and the lives they actually lived varied greatly. They thought that by *acting* perfect they could honor God and inspire perfection.

Now it was my turn. Would my audience be impressed with me? No, there was no reason for them to be impressed. Instead, I wanted them to feel safe. I wanted them to feel free to let their guard down so that the Word of God could penetrate their hearts. I wanted to disarm them by letting them know I wasn't going to intimidate or hurt them. I had learned that when an audience can identify with the *messenger,* they will more readily identify with the *message.*

I openly shared the Word that God had made flesh in my life. I shared the good, the bad and the ugly. For it is truly the areas where we have been weak that God will anoint with His strength. Tears streaked their cheeks as I spoke, because it was no longer my voice that they heard, but the Voice within my voice. They recognized in me their own fears and failures. Encouraged by my honesty, they in turn were honest with themselves. I was a mirror that reflected their own fears and struggles. Because they identified with me, they could more easily believe that if God had done it for me, then

He would certainly do it for them.

At the close of the meeting, these women flooded the altar with tears of joy and repentance. I joined them there as we wept in awe of the sweet and tangible presence of God. We had brought our hearts before Him, and He had accepted our offerings.

COURAGE TO STEP OUT

It is in this same spirit that I write these words. It is not because I think I know it all. *I don't.* I write because I believe with all my heart that it is God's mandate on my life to share the things He has taught me. I write to you because I know you are not so different from me. We face similar struggles, pain and triumphs. It is not my goal to tell you what to do, but to accompany you on a search. We are sisters, although I have no biological sisters.

I will share very openly and honestly. Pretense and appearances are void of power and cannot help anyone. Teachings without the practical knowledge of how to apply them do nothing but weigh us down.

Therefore, I commit to hide nothing from you that I feel might help you. You will have the advantage of gleaning from my foolishness, mishaps and mistakes.

In return, I ask that you dare to do the same. Dare to be open and honest with yourself. What we hide eventually ensnares and imprisons us. It grows strongest in the shadows of shame and condemnation.

> We must summon the courage as individuals and step out from behind the facades where we have hidden ourselves.

The gospel we preach extends beyond the eternal hope we have because Jesus rose from the dead and restored mankind to God. It is a gospel that empowers us as we live here and now, and its truth will invade every area where we allow Christ to impact us and change our lives.

We must summon the courage as individuals

and step out from behind the facades where we have hidden ourselves. Even in the church, some act as though they never really needed a Savior. The truth is, we all have sinned and fallen short. Our closets are cluttered and full.

Some like it that way. They like the feel of all that clutter. They feel safe holding on to the past. They will tell you they don't have room for any more, because their closets are already bursting at the seams, and they will insist that they already know everything they need to know. They are satisfied with what they have.

> He who is full loathes honey, but to the hungry even what is bitter tastes sweet.
> —Proverbs 27:7

Cleaning out the misinformation and clutter of the world from our lives may appear bitter. But we will find, as we empty ourselves of what only temporarily satisfies, that we will have an appetite for more. If we remain full, even the honey of God's wisdom will seem unappetizing. Just like a second round of dessert after you have already eaten a Thanksgiving banquet, what looked so good at the beginning of the meal now causes you to groan in discomfort just looking at it.

I believe you are hungry, and that is why you are giving the gift of your time in order to read this book. I believe you want more than what you've had, and are therefore willing to give more of yourself to God.

QUESTIONS

So here are a few more questions for you to answer. Again, bear in mind that this is not a test. I am going to ask these questions in the figurative terms of closet cleaning, but it is the heart's storage with which we are actually dealing. These questions are simply so we can locate your heart. For privacy, your answers can be recorded on a separate piece of paper or inside a journal.

1. Are you intimidated by the thought of cleaning out the closet of your mind?
2. Even so, are you ready to do it?

(I made the first two simple *yes/no* questions so you could prove to yourself you could do it!)

3. What are some things you think you might find inside your closet that need to be thrown away? Please be specific. List any stained items from your past that need to be discarded.

4. What are some valuable articles that you need to pass on? Remember those maternity clothes. Recount God's proven faithfulness.

5. With whom would you like to share these items?

6. Are there items that need to be laundered in God's forgiveness?

7. Are you ashamed of the clutter in your closet?

8. Are you ready to make room for the new by tossing out the old?

Adapted from *The True Measure of a Woman*, 9–20.

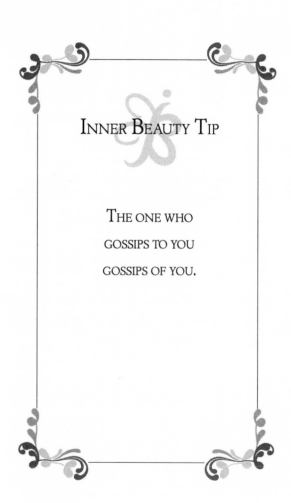

INNER BEAUTY TIP

THE ONE WHO
GOSSIPS TO YOU
GOSSIPS OF YOU.

3

Gossip: More Than Mere Words

Without wood a fire goes out; without gossip a quarrel dies down.

—PROVERBS 26:20

As a member of a sorority in college I discovered the danger of reentering a room you had just left. Nine times out of ten, when you walked back in you'd catch your sorority sisters discussing your vices or virtues. I always took great pains to remember everything I needed before leaving the room. If necessity warranted my return, I tried to make noise in the hall before I opened the door.

It was always painful and embarrassing to hear whispers or laughter suddenly become silent as I walked back in the room for that toothbrush or towel I'd forgotten. I'd scan their faces and know—partly because of the sick feeling in my own stomach—they had just dined on some juicy tidbit.

This was to be expected. In my sorority very few girls claimed to be Christians. I boldly proclaimed myself a heathen committed to the pursuit of pleasure and protection of self! I sought pleasure for the moment and protection from future pain. So I was not above gossiping. I looked at it as self-defense. I mean, women gossip, right?

Then, during the summer between my junior and senior years, to the shock and utter disbelief of all those around me, this heathen became a Christian. Another student on campus led me in the sinner's prayer, and I accepted Jesus as my Lord and Savior. (That young man would later become my husband.) I was gloriously saved, liberated from alcohol and instantly healed of severe lactose intolerance. (This hereditary disorder caused me to be hospitalized two months earlier due to a severe reaction to a dairy product. After we said a simple prayer, I was able to eat pizza, milk shakes and all the other things that had caused me severe pain since my teen years.) It was then that I understood why my shallow, self-centered lifestyle had left me feeling empty.

When I returned to school I found my old surroundings hard to reconcile with my newfound faith. I felt God was leading me to move to Dallas. John, the young man who had shared Christ with me, was there, and I was excited to join a church and be welcomed by my new and true sisters.

Sister Talk

It will be altogether different now! I thought. *The women in church are Christians.* I imagined smiling Christian friends welcoming me with open arms and older women who would disciple me.

Boy, was I in for a shock! They were not the least bit happy to see me. I was not welcomed; instead, given the already low population of eligible Christian bachelors, I was viewed as a competitive threat.

That first Sunday I felt their disapproval as they sized me up from a distance, studying my appearance and demeanor. They were politely cool as I was introduced, then quickly turned the conversation to subjects or persons of which I had no knowledge. For the first time since becoming a Christian I felt strangely awkward.

I imagined smiling Christian friends welcoming me with open arms and older women who would disciple me.

Judging by the looks I received, I thought it was quite possible they doubted that my conversion was genuine. I had been saved only a few months and had not yet assembled a "sanctified" wardrobe. I owned the wardrobe of a sorority party girl. I had no money to purchase new clothes, so I set about trying to convince them that despite my appearance I was sincere and my intentions honorable. The boys were friendly, but the girls remained distant and distrustful.

Oh well, I thought. *Maybe God doesn't want me to have any girls for friends.*

I built a facade to hide how I really lived.

John had proposed a few months before I arrived in Dallas, but I was not ready to be engaged. All my life I had measured myself by whom I had dated or by my family's social status. Now I wanted to get to know my Father God. I knew God had called me to marry John, but I decided not to date him. I continued school, worked and attended church. I was careful to come to church late, sit alone and leave early. I reasoned that this gave the impression of a fulfilled and busy life. I built a facade to hide how I really lived.

The truth is I was extremely lonely. I had never been alone, and in this solitude I questioned my wisdom in leaving school. I had been starry-eyed and idealistic. It appeared that my sorority contained more warmth, hospitality and compassion than I found in the church. At least I knew what to expect from my sorority sisters. These people totally confused me. I was baffled by this reception from my real spiritual sisters.

I spent hours crying to my mother, who was a Christian by that time. With my decision to leave the university and attend a Christian college, my father stopped covering my expenses. I was alone in a one-room apartment with no friends, furniture or money. I had gone from a rich party girl with lots of friends and social engagements to a poor lonely person living off part-time waitress tips.

One Sunday as I tried to slip out of church unnoticed I met a young man my age. We laughed and talked for a while, and a few weeks later we went to dinner. About an hour into our meal he blurted out, "You're really not as bad as they say!"

I was astonished. I was certain the reason I had been ignored was because my presence went unnoticed. "As bad as who says?" I questioned.

"Well, you know," he stammered, "all the other girls and my aunt."

My surprise turned to horror! All the other girls *and his aunt!* She happened to be one of the most influential and prominent women in this five-thousand-member church.

It seemed the women had decided I was conceited. They also were toying with the idea that I had cast a spell of some sort on John so that he would not date anyone. That was why he told everyone he was going to marry me.

Heartbroken, I went home, certain my desire to obey God and leave school was all a mistake. I cried myself to sleep.

LET GOD DO THE TALKING

But the next morning at service my sorrow turned to anger as I watched this prominent woman ascend the platform to share something God had laid on her heart. I clenched my fists as I tried to remain composed until she was finished.

As soon as church was over, I dashed for my car. Alone with my thoughts, I consoled myself. *I wonder what people would think if they knew what Mrs. High-and-Mighty was really like?*

I was contemplating who and what to tell when I was interrupted by the gentle voice of God. "Lisa, if you defend yourself, I will not defend you."

"But God, it's not true!" I argued.

"If you start defending yourself now," He answered, "you will have to do it for the rest of your life." Then He gave me His promise, "If you will not defend yourself, I will be your defense."

I knew my situation was hopeless. Whom could I tell anyway? I knew no one in Dallas except those who had maligned me. I was twenty-one years old with no influence, friends or money.

> # "If you will not defend yourself, I will be your defense."

God questioned me, "Lisa, do you know what gossip is?"

I was certain I did, so I answered, "People talking about others irresponsibly."

The Lord gave me a deeper definition. "Gossip is two or more people standing in agreement with the lies of the devil."

"But what if it is true?" I questioned, thinking of what the woman at church did to me. I only wanted to tell the truth about her.

In answer, God described a scenario I could

understand. "What if you saw a Christian woman leave a bar on the arm of a man and go home and spend the night with him? What would you think?"

I answered the obvious.

He continued, "Would you be right if you repeated it?"

I felt certain that if I had been an eyewitness and my information was accurate, then it would be all right to repeat it.

"What if she confessed and repented of her sin?" He asked. "What would happen then? What would I do with her iniquity?"

I answered, "You would bury it in the sea of forgetfulness, as far as the east is from the west" (Ps. 103:12).

"Then as far as I would be concerned, it had never happened. If I had forgotten it, then you would have no right to repeat it, would you?"

"No," I answered, "I would have no right."

In this incident God was faithful to defend me. This woman even took me to lunch eventually and apologized to me herself. But first God had me go to her, humble myself and apologize for acting aloof (remember my feigned busy life). At lunch she confessed she did not know why she had singled me out to gossip about. She said that now she would blow her trumpet just as loudly about what a wonderful young lady I was.

SWEET NOTHINGS

Gossip can be extremely painful. At one time or another, all of us have suffered from the wounds of careless words. We have felt the isolation and rejection they bring. We have seen the averted eyes and sensed the distance in others' measured words, words that often carried additional unspoken messages. We have known the turned backs of those who have avoided us.

Gossip is the Godiva chocolate of conversation. What it lacks in nutritional value it makes up for in taste.

Perhaps someone with whom you have shared your heart in openness and vulnerability is now closed off to you. You feel as if you were locked out and are not sure why.

All of us can identify with the pain, so why would any of us gossip?

For the most part women are communicators. To some of us, talking is as necessary as eating! Talking is how we sort through information and problems. It is a gift to be able to communicate love, concern, humor and information verbally. It is equally important to use this gift to help others express their deeper feelings and fears. Women are gifted with the ability to surround others with warm words and a supportive atmosphere. This is healthy and necessary. But gossip is not a healthy part of this balanced diet.

Gossip is the Godiva chocolate of conversation. What it lacks in nutritional value it makes up for in taste. Like chocolate, it is tasty, costly and exhilarating for the moment—and void of constructive nutrition. After an initial high you are left with a headache. You know you shouldn't have another morsel, but it tasted so good!

King Solomon described the attraction of gossip this way:

> The words of a talebearer are like tasty trifles, and they go down into the inmost body.
>
> —PROVERBS 18:8, NKJV

These are highly descriptive words. The words *tasty trifles* describe something that is delicious and indulgent but minuscule. It is an overdressed little thing—a bit of information or conversation that was assigned too much importance. Unfortunately, this overdressed trivia has the power to penetrate deep into the soul.

The dictionary defines *gossip* as "rumor, defamation, hearsay, scandal, chatter, news, slander." The act of *gossiping* is described as "to tattle, blab, chatter, noise or tale bear." It is interesting to note that truth is not mentioned anywhere in the definition of gossip. Gossip is a negligent scattering of ungrounded accusations and misrepresentations. It has no credibility or accountability. It is secretive and selective, and its real agenda is always well hidden.

THE JEALOUSY FACTOR

We become the prey of jealousy when we mistakenly believe God's favor toward one person indicates His disfavor toward us. Remember Cain? His was the first account of jealousy in the Bible. He perceived Abel's acceptance as his rejection. Unfortunately, even today jealousy is rampant among Christian brethren.

> We become the prey of jealousy when we mistakenly believe God's favor toward one person indicates His disfavor toward us.

Jealousy breeds competition, which is fueled by gossip. In this arena gossip is not limited to quiet whispers behind someone's back but includes open and public (or even pulpit) slander from others. Those with power and influence will often use it to try to defame those they perceive as threats to their success. Jealousy is a very ugly and consuming fear. There are those who curse their brethren out of jealousy, and it is important to be prepared to respond by blessing them.

Covetousness, desiring what God has given another, is an offspring of jealousy. I never saw myself as someone who would covet until I watched God bless another person with something I needed.

When we first began to travel, we crossed the United States with our three small children packed into a Honda Civic. Every night our family would join hands to pray. In faith we would thank God for our new van.

In the course of our travels we visited a church where a couple had just been given a van. Though I was happy for them, I was not happy for me! I really needed a van! The couple who received the van attended the church where we ministered. They had fewer children and didn't even travel. God just gave them a van. They were so excited as they shared how God had blessed them. They even admitted they did not really need it.

I thought for certain there had been a mistake. Surely whoever gave it to them was supposed to have given it to me. I knew my reaction was wrong, but I thought, *It is not fair!*

Discouraged, I complained to God about it. My need was greater, so why did He give it to them?

He answered me, "Lisa, you are upset because you see their blessing as a deduction from My ability to bless you. It did not come from your account but Mine. I am unlimited."

> We are tempted to gossip when we perceive someone else's favor, provision or position as a deduction from God's ability to bless, protect or provide for us.

Of course God was right. I perceived their blessing as a rejection of my need. Instead of rejoicing with them I had allowed jealousy to turn my focus back to me.

I imagined God's provision as a big storehouse that now contained one less van. I reasoned that their blessing had diminished God's ability to supply for me. They had upset my odds of winning!

We are tempted to gossip when we perceive someone else's favor, provision or position as a deduction from God's ability to bless, protect or provide for us.

DRAWING OTHERS TO OURSELVES

Jealousy will even manifest itself in friendships. Perhaps God has blessed us with a friend, but we are not certain of the security of this friendship. Because of this we are tempted to discredit anything or anyone we perceive as a threat to this relationship. We malign others to gain the allegiance of our friend. Friendships based on foundations such as this will never last long because soon we become possessive and jealous. We will be offended by the very friend we tried to secure because we perceive any attention our friend gives to another as disloyalty to us.

It is imperative, especially in these times, that we allow God to establish our friendship based on His truth and principles. First make God your best friend.

He who loves a pure heart and whose speech

50

is gracious will have the king for his friend.
—PROVERBS 22:11

Then let the King choose your friends.

We must desire pure hearts over our need for friendships. Part of purifying our hearts is refining our speech. Our words are to be gracious or filled with grace. Grace has been described in two different ways:

1. The ability to do what truth demands
2. Unmerited favor

We must desire pure hearts over our need for friendships.

Both of these apply to our friendships. To speak graciously requires honoring or covering those who in our estimation don't deserve it. But isn't that what God does for us? He covers us by His blood and honors us with His name. Likewise, we are to cover and honor those around us whether or not we feel they deserve it. God will choose *His* friends for us, and thus He will want us to treat them the way He would treat them. Then God will entrust us with true friends because He knows we will be true to them.

TAKE HEED WHAT YOU HEAR

So far we have discussed gossip in terms of what we say, but gossip is not limited to what is spoken. Often the most difficult and destructive gossip to shake is not what you have said but what you have heard.

> A wicked man listens to evil lips; a liar pays attention to a malicious tongue.
> —PROVERBS 17:4

The Bible calls it wicked even to listen to malicious lips. Perhaps you listened to others and thought it was all right because you did not agree with what you heard. You just wanted them to be able to air their grievances to someone safe. Well, it is not safe for them, and it is definitely not safe for you!

As you listened, your own soul was defiled by what you heard. Unknowingly, you now watch for the discussed attributes or character flaws in the accused individual. Amazingly, your eyes are open, and you can see clearly what had been hidden before. You think it is because you are more discerning now. No, it's because you are more suspicious.

Suddenly, whenever you hear that individual's name mentioned, your mind sings the chorus of accusations and complaints you heard earlier. Soon you are wrestling with your own critical thoughts toward that person. You are tempted to judge his or her motives and actions.

This is especially dangerous with leaders and marriage partners.

Listening to gossip about leaders undermines those whom God has placed over us (bosses, parents, teachers or ministers). We become distrustful of the very ones God has put in our lives to guide, provide, train or minister to us.

The gossip we hear is dangerous to our marriage because it cuts off our intimacy. We don't feel free to give ourselves to our partner when we are afraid he may hurt us. It is important when someone comes to you with a complaint about your mate that you make that person aware that you and your mate are one.

In the early years of ministry a few women took me to lunch. One began to tell me how much she liked me, but she felt my husband was too extreme. She cited her reasons and began to criticize John.

I interrupted her. "Please forgive me if I ever gave you the impression that I did not agree with or support John in this position. I do. By speaking against him you are speaking against me. So you can address your complaints to me directly." She immediately stopped. She was more interested in criticizing than in solving anything.

Be careful. Don't allow others, even family members, to criticize your mate and undermine your unity. Discern whether they are trying to be constructive or destructive. Often they are unaware of the damaging effect of their words. They think that by pointing out a problem they are giving you answers. Gently correct them.

WHAT ARE WE TO DO?

I have just given a sampling of some gossip pitfalls. I have been open with you so that you will in turn be honest with yourself.

Every time I gossiped I was grieved and vowed never to do it again. This was a constant source of frustration for me. I knew in my heart I did not want to do it, yet it seemed impossible for me to stop. I repented of one scenario only to be caught up in another. It got to the place where I asked God to isolate me until I was able to rise above this pattern or stronghold in my life.

> ## To rid yourself of the fruit of gossip you must first destroy the tree.

Why had a stronghold been established in my life, and why was it so hard to overcome? Picture an orchard with many rows of fruit trees in your backyard. One row of trees consistently produces bad fruit. The fruit from the trees in this row is diseased and infested with insects and worms. You don't want the pestilence of the bad fruit to spread to your good trees, so weekly you work your way down the row picking off the diseased fruit in order to burn it. But as soon as you've finished the last tree in the row you notice bad fruit has reappeared on the first tree. Frustrated, you start the whole process over.

To accomplish this you must neglect the care of your good trees and their harvest of fruit. The good trees are laden with good fruit, but you are too busy plucking off the bad fruit to harvest it.

To rid yourself of the fruit of gossip you must first destroy the tree. It is useless and frustrating to waste your time destroying the fruit. You need to take an ax to the root that is nourishing the tree and feeding the fruit. These roots are drawing on something that is destroying your fruit.

Gossip is rooted in unbelief and watered by fear. We already know that fear is a spirit and unbelief is a condition of the heart. Therefore we could certainly call gossip a heart condition.

We fall prey to gossip when we are afraid to trust God to uphold us in truth. No matter how complex or unique our situation is, if we are honest we will find fear and unbelief at the root.

We don't forgive because we fear being hurt

again. So we stand guard over past offenses. In doing so we prove that we doubt God's ability to heal our past and protect our futures.

We malign others because we believe our worth is tied to theirs. We're afraid that if they look good we'll look worse by comparison. This reveals that our self-worth is not founded in Jesus Christ.

Gossip is rooted in unbelief and watered by fear.

We are jealous because we do not believe God is just. We are afraid He actually plays favorites and honors people instead of faith and obedience. We must remember that anything we receive is by grace and faith in God's goodness.

Healing the Wounds of Gossip

> Reckless words pierce like a sword, but the tongue of the wise brings healing.
> —Proverbs 12:18

Gossip is reckless or careless words that wound.

57

The only way to heal the wounds is to speak words in answer that contain wisdom and promote reconciliation. We are not to answer in the same manner the information was brought to us. An example of such an answer would be to agree with the gossiper and offer our own story about how the offender hurt us also. This would not bring healing. We are instructed:

> Do not answer a fool according to his folly, or you will be like him yourself.
> —PROVERBS 26:4

> He who covers over an offense promotes love, but whoever repeats the matter separates close friends.
> —PROVERBS 17:9

When we listen to a repeated offense it can separate us from our closest friends. These verses are referring to a hurt or wound from someone close to us. We must develop the wisdom and discernment necessary to answer with words of life. I have found Proverbs to be an excellent source of wisdom to govern my heart.

It is difficult to safeguard yourself from this

type of gossip, but it helps if you ask yourself these questions:

- Why are they telling me this?

- Are they confessing their reaction to the offenses or just repeating it to influence me?

- Have they gone to the individual who offended them?

- Are they asking me to go with them so restoration can take place?

- Am I in a position to help them?

If the answers to these questions are unclear, you are not the one to whom they should be speaking. They should first speak with the one who offended them.

By studying Proverbs and rehearsing these questions, we will not only be able to answer with wisdom, but we will also rightly divide our own thoughts and motives. This will carry over when we go to others with our grievances.

BROADSIDED

Be wary of those things that will weaken your defenses against gossiping. When someone comes to you for counsel, she may intentionally or unknowingly flatter you. This causes you to lose your discernment.

> Do not accept a bribe, for a bribe blinds those who see and twists the words of the righteous.
>
> —EXODUS 23:8

It is unlikely that someone is going to slip you a twenty-dollar bill. The type of bribe you must guard against is flattery that comes by way of comments such as, "I knew I could bring this to you because you won't tell anyone." This makes us feel trustworthy and as if we are in an exclusive relationship with this person. Under the influence of this type of flattery, I have promised not to repeat matters that would have been better brought into the open. Trustworthiness is proven in time. We can never be certain of the facts until we have heard the whole matter.

Someone may flatter you by saying, "I know

you are godly and discerning."

I once received a call from a woman who said she'd heard I had the ability to interpret dreams. Then she proceeded to tell me not only her dream, but also the interpretation. As a result of her dream she had concluded that her pastor was not a man of the Spirit. In actuality she was not asking me anything. She was simply telling me something on which she wanted my agreement and support. Be careful whom you listen to.

Those who carry stories *to* you carry stories *from* you.

When I was a child, there was a precious Irish-Catholic family with eight children who lived around the corner from me. Their mother had decorated her kitchen in a unique way. She had hand-painted assorted proverbs on the walls. I remember one of them distinctly: "He who gossips to you gossips of you."

Experientially, I have found this proverb to be

true. Those who carry stories *to* you carry stories *from* you. They will often mention your name by association. "I was at lunch with Lisa the other day. Did you know so-and-so said such and such?" All the other person remembers is your name and the comment. You are now guilty by association.

SPEAK THE TRUTH

We have to rise up and become people who are willing to be bold enough to see through the flattery of man and speak the truth. By merely listening we validate an offense. We must ask God for the wisdom to speak His restoration and truth. When we attack each other we are warned:

> If you keep on biting and devouring each other, watch out or you will be destroyed by each other.
>
> —GALATIANS 5:15

Why should Satan battle us when he can have us do it for him? Remember, he has been stripped of his weapons. He wants us to be the accuser of the brethren for him. By waging war against each other we fulfill his purpose. It is time to build up, not destroy each other. It is important not to align ourselves with the lies of the enemy, but with the truth of our Father.

What we view as innocent and well-meaning God has a way of revealing for what it really is. When we ask Him to separate the precious from the vile, He points out our hidden flaws and holds them at arm's length to allow us to scrutinize them by His light. His all-revealing light offers a much different perspective than does the dim illumination of our intentions. It is at this point that we see our flaws for what they really are—horrific.

Though we may be tempted to make excuses for our behavior, it is crucial to let the pain and shame of this revelation pierce our hearts at the moment we gossip. Then we will turn to our loving Father and ask His forgiveness, renounce our involvement with gossip and rejoice as God hurls it away. If we make the mistake of justifying our behavior, we will find ourselves held captive to it.

Adapted from Lisa Bevere *Out of Control and Loving It!*, 131–147.

INNER BEAUTY TIP

IF ALLOWED, THE DEMANDS
AND PRESSURES AROUND YOU
WILL ALWAYS USURP
YOUR PRIORITIES AND
DISORDER YOUR DAY.

4

Self-Denial or Self-Neglect

> But seek first his kingdom and his right-
> eousness, and all these things will be given
> to you as well.
>
> —MATTHEW 6:33

veryone needs something from me! These words are often uttered through clenched teeth when we feel pulled in every direction. Yet if we are honest, this complaining is accompanied by a sense of self-satisfaction. Things could be worse—what if no one needed us? What if our labor and talent were unnoticed by those around us?

Even in our exasperation we find comfort because we are needed. We sigh and quickly reassure those around us that we can manage our unbearable loads. Why?

To be effective for Christ we must know what we are to accomplish—the purpose for which we were created.

Because women need to be needed, and men need to be respected. Women are compassionate. It is in our very nature to aid and assist. It is very important that a woman feel indispensable and irreplaceable. To assure this prominence she will often position herself in the lives of her loved ones as the "need-meeter."

But are we the need-meeters? God designed women to nurture and nurse their husbands, children and loved ones. But what empowers us can become a drain to us if we try to meet all the needs in our own strengths and abilities. Sometimes we are so busy meeting needs that we forget we have needs of our own. Busyness can be our greatest enemy.

Without realizing it, women often tend to elevate whatever need is set before them to a position of priority. This is appropriate in the case of emergencies, and it is important to be flexible and spontaneous to a degree. But when the exception becomes a lifestyle it is destructive.

To be effective for Christ we must know what we are to accomplish—the purpose for which we were created. Without priorities in place we will move through our days without purpose, hoping we're going in the right direction.

If allowed, the demands and pressures around us will always usurp our priorities and disorder our days. Soon insignificant crises, interruptions and phone calls have blown us off course. Then activity without purpose navigates our lives. This upheaval wears us out. Our days will be filled with busyness but very little productivity. This drains us and causes us to feel like a failure. This steals our joy and, with it, our strength.

My Frustrating Routine

To explain, I want to share some examples from my own life. I often had a hard time accepting help from others. I felt guilty, reasoning that I really should be able to handle it on my own. I thought, *If only I was more organized or got up earlier, I could do it all.* If someone offered to help me, I felt pressured to return the help by entertaining the person or ministering to him or her in some way to appease the guilt of my own inadequacies.

It was easier to do it all myself. But I was constantly distracted and drained of energy. I allowed everyone else's needs to set my priorities.

I spent my days running in circles—responding to this crisis, starting that project, interrupted by another crisis—until I was utterly frustrated and determined just to survive until my children's bedtime when I would get a break.

I'd tuck my last child in around 10 P.M. Then I'd come alive. I could finally accomplish something with the children asleep and the phone quiet. I knew I would not be interrupted. As the rest of the world prepared for bed, I started a load of laundry and headed for the kitchen.

With small boys and a husband who is often gone, I find that my kitchen can be terrifying. I set to work cleaning up the feast of dropped food under the table, then decide I needed to tackle the entire kitchen floor. I had white tile floors and white grout, and keeping it that way is a real challenge. I'd get out the bleach and scouring powder and scrub it with a toothbrush until I felt I was going to pass out from bleach fumes. Then I'd head upstairs to our office to write out checks to pay the bills. It was always between 1 A.M. and 2 A.M. by the time I tumbled into bed.

At 6:30 A.M. the whole cycle started again. I'd stumble into my kitchen to start a coffee IV. My children would watch with a mixture of pity and curiosity. They understood (because I had told them many times) that moms do things for hours while everyone else sleeps.

My oldest son once asked innocently, "Why don't you just go to bed?"

"I can't. Who would do everything?" I explained.

"Oh," he nodded sadly.

I'd listen to my children's bedtime prayers, and my second son prayed regularly, "God, let Mommy be fresh in the morning." But I never was.

So they'd watch helplessly as I'd wander the

kitchen from counter to counter like a pinball, trying to pack lunch and make breakfast. I'd rush my oldest son off to school, clean up the kitchen and attempt to get in the shower before the phone started ringing—but I'd never quite make it. It was 9 A.M. and the rest of the world was already awake and showered.

I'd become frustrated with the interruptions, usually getting out of the shower just in time to start lunch. After lunch I'd only get an hour's worth of work done before it was time to pick up the kids from school.

Such was my daily cycle.

While pregnant with my fourth son I became anemic. My husband put his foot down. He made me hire a cleaning lady to come in twice a month. It helped, but during the other two weeks in the month the messes would not wait.

One night when I was four months pregnant, I was down on my hands and knees scrubbing my tile floor at midnight. I proudly gloated to myself, *No cleaning lady gets my floor this clean. No one gets this grout as white as I do.*

God interrupted me, "Lisa, when you stand

before Me I am not going to reward you because you cleaned your own tile floor the best. You'll be rewarded by how faithful you were with what I told you to do. Let all this little stuff go." Suddenly my boasting seemed so stupid, my exhaustion so useless. I already knew what would happen the next morning. I would wake up tired and grumpy, running behind before my day even began.

I was deriving my self-worth from something other than God.

But I was stubborn. I received my self-worth by doing all these things. I enjoyed being viewed as a martyr by my family. I reasoned, *I'll just get up at 6 a.m. and take my shower before my children are up so I can be more organized. Then I can continue doing all my housework, the administration of the ministry and care for the children.* So I continued to do everything and still found myself running behind.

I was deriving my self-worth from something

other than God. I derived it from my selfless labor for my family. But in fact, I was not selfless. I was selfish to withhold from them what really mattered—my time and attention.

NEGLECTING SELF AND FAMILY

In the fifth month of my pregnancy my car was hit from behind. The baby was fine, but now I was pregnant and suffering from whiplash. I was no longer physically able to do all the busy stuff. I had to face my physical limitations and distorted perceptions. Finally I threw up my hands and hired a cleaning lady to come every week until I had the baby.

Why did I wait until I was totally incapacitated before I gave up? Because I was busy and troubled with many things. I had confused self-denial with self-neglect. I thought by caring for everyone but me I was denying myself. It made me feel needed and spiritual. But in truth I was denying my family; I was denying God's call on my life; and I was neglecting myself.

Self-denial is laying down our natural will to choose to pursue God's purpose.

Then Jesus said to his disciples, "If anyone
would come after me, he must deny himself
and take up his cross and follow me."
—MATTHEW 16:24

I denied my children a rested, pleasantly awake
mother in the morning. I denied my husband and
children quality time with me because I was always
tense and distracted. I felt the need to labor end-
lessly because I was under the constant weight of
all I had yet to finish.

Self-denial is laying down our natural will to choose to pursue God's purpose.

When my husband was home I denied him a
wife in bed with him because of my wacky schedule. I stayed up much later than he did or sneaked
out of the room once he was asleep. I denied my
children access to me. Unintentionally, I pushed
them aside when I allowed every phone call to
interrupt our time together. Then I rushed them

off to bed. I was not enjoying my husband and children—I was surviving them!

MARTHA MOM

I had become a Martha mom. I deprived myself of sleep, exercise and recreation. I neglected the joy of my marriage and children. For what reason? To take care of "things."

Worst of all, I neglected myself spiritually, always giving out and never taking in. This neglect was not for spiritual gain but for mommy busyness. I was such a Martha! I'd get down on the floor to pray and notice a Lego under the sofa. After putting it away I discovered something else amiss. Soon I was cleaning the entire upstairs, totally forgetting I had knelt down to pray.

> "Martha, Martha," the Lord answered, "you are worried and upset about many things, but only one thing is needed. Mary has chosen what is better, and it will not be taken away from her."
>
> —LUKE 10:41–42

Sometimes we just have to let the Legos lie,

close our eyes, tune out all that would distract us and press in to God. At first this may seem more difficult than cleaning. We are used to activity. That's how we feel needed. Martha wanted Mary in the kitchen laboring over the food preparation. Mary had the attitude, "I can eat later; right now Jesus is talking, and I want to hear Him." Our time of prayer, praise or worship is not another demand the Lord places on us. It is something He provides for our refreshing.

> When we busy ourselves with the temporary to the neglect of the eternal, we become frustrated.

I used to view prayer as just one more thing I had not accomplished at the end of my day. I did pray every day, but I wanted to have two full hours in the closet (which I'm sure I would have begun to straighten). At the end of the day when I was finally able to squeeze in a few minutes with God, I thought He was upset because I hadn't given Him two hours earlier, so I would spend my prayer time apologizing. One day He interrupted my condemnation report. "This is for you!" He said. "Stop seeing Me as angry at you for not coming earlier. I am glad we are together now. Let Me refresh you so you will look forward to these times together." This revolutionized my outlook on prayer.

When we busy ourselves with the temporary to the neglect of the eternal, we become frustrated. We blame those around us even though our frustration is due to a lack of our own refreshing. We are not refreshed because we are too busy taking care of everything so others can be refreshed. Then we get mad at them when they are not running at our hectic pace, and we are still frantically banging pots and pans in the kitchen. We need to throw down our pots and pans and enjoy God and each other.

God showed me that I could experience the same refreshing I received in His presence as I spent time with my husband and children. I had become too busy being a mother to be a nurturer. Too busy being a wife to be a companion. After all, I felt I proved my love by meeting needs.

When John asked me to go golfing with him, I replied, "I don't have time to golf!" I was irritated that he did.

The truth was I had time for what I made time for. But I had not allotted any time for recreation or enjoyment. I was so driven to care for the ones I loved that I had forgotten to enjoy them.

Remember, God made us for companionship. He gave the woman to the man so the man would not be alone. He wanted them to enjoy each other and all that He had created for them. When we replace our time of fellowship with Him with the works of our hands, we are spent of our strength.

The same is true of children and friends. If we do not spend time developing these relationships they will eventually quit growing.

How can we safeguard our time from this theft? How can we keep our perspective correct? What should our priorities be? I know there are already many good books on how to order your day, time and priorities. One advises this order: God, husband, children, job, church, yourself. Another recommends: God, yourself, ministry, husband, children, church, job, friends. I'm not going to attempt to compile a list for fear it would be used as a formula.

I don't believe a formula exists! If it did, it certainly would not be found within my wisdom. The longer I walk with God, the more I realize that formulas, rules and laws lead inevitably to the path of religion. Just ask yourself, What is my motive?

FOR WHAT ARE YOU LABORING?

You can never correctly order your priorities until they've been assigned value and worth. I'm not referring to *time management* as much as I am to *heart management*.

The children of Israel wanted a list of rules and formulas more than a relationship with their Creator. They had every possible detail spelled out for them on how to obey God and stay holy. But it didn't work.

Jesus summed it up this way:

> Love the Lord your God with all your heart and with all your soul and with all your mind…Love your neighbor as yourself.
> —MATTHEW 22:37–39

He took away lifeless, rigid structure. He did not tell them how to love God and their neighbors. Jesus knew that if their hearts were pure, then their actions would follow.

What is our value structure? Can we be trusted to create one? No, because our very nature is to be busy and distracted, not only at home but also at church and at our jobs. We cannot trust ourselves to measure accurately the merit of what God has placed in our care.

> ## Jesus knew that if their hearts were pure, then their actions would follow.

We live in a world whose standard is relative. It drifts on a sea of uncertainty and constant change. This standard shifts and slides with the rise and fall of each wave. Good is bad, and bad is good. This floating morality does not value or esteem what God esteems. Our culture rewards achievement and appearance, but God rewards faithfulness and substance.

Things Are Not What They Seem

Unfortunately, many a Christian is busy laboring to appear to be someone of substance and accomplishment. This leaves the person feeling void and fearful. Appearances are very laborious to maintain. Any strength that person yields is expended in their constant protection. Appearances drain us of the energy we need to change.

Appearance by definition means "presentation, air, bearing, semblance or demeanor." In contrast, *substance* is defined as "the essence, matter, element or material." This definition suggests the very life or truth of an issue, person or thing. What it is made of, not merely what it is cloaked in.

God's ways are higher than our own. The truth always outlives a lie.

The truth is not ashamed; it is open and rides

the winds of principles that supersede time. Appearances merely cover over the outward and gain their strength through deception. Time is the captor of appearance, and ultimately time exposes and destroys it. God's ways are higher than our own. His truth and principles live on. The truth always outlives a lie.

I challenge you to examine your lifestyle honestly. Are you so busy you neglect yourself and those you love? Have you mistaken self-neglect for self-denial? For what are you laboring? Are you drawing your security from the little things, or have you focused on the eternal?

If your answer to any of these questions is *yes,* don't use them as an excuse for a guilt trip. Instead, let them motivate you to change.

Adapted from *Out of Control and Loving It!,* 149–157.

Conclusion

I write with an urgency in my spirit. The time will come, whether it is near or far, when each of us must individually stand before the holy God of the universe. It is imperative that we change our perspective from a temporal one to an eternal one. We must understand our true measure from an eternal point of view.

This will not be easily accomplished, as there is an aggressive onslaught against this wisdom of eternity. The spirit of this world has lulled many of us into a false sense of security and comfort. It has encouraged us to compare ourselves with each other and with the world. But the standard by which we will be measured will not include these factors.

Pursue Him, for
He alone bears the image
that radiates God's glory.

Our standard is our Master and Lord, Jesus Christ. It is one of unattainable holiness only found in those who are hid in Christ. Pursue Him, for He alone bears the image that radiates God's glory. Behold Him, and you will be changed and transformed by the power of the Holy Spirit into His likeness. Only then will you radiate the inner beauty of a woman of God—His beauty, His glory. His glory is the measure of your worth. This visage blends faith, love and holy fear. It opens blind eyes and deaf ears. It transforms hearts of stone into tender hearts of flesh. If you want to know this Lord and Savior from the depths of your being, pray this prayer. I caution you—do not pray this prayer until you are ready to lay down your own life and take up His.

Dearest Father God, You are so holy, I

cannot even look upon You, let alone approach You. In Your wisdom and mercy, You provided a perfect sacrifice, one that would cover the very deepest and darkest hidden sin in my life. You gave Your only Son in sacrifice that I might live. Though I am unworthy of this, Your love for me superseded my judgment.

I lay my own life at Your feet and repent of my former life of sin and self-ishness. Jesus, I embrace the cross and lay down my will that I might fulfill Yours. Wash me, and I will be clean before You. I make You Lord of my life and Savior of my soul. I leave behind the kingdom of darkness as I now enter Your kingdom of light.

Show me the true measure of my worth to You. Help me to be the woman of God You created me to be. Amen.

Adapted from *The True Measure of a Woman*, 171–172.

If you are enjoying the Inner Beauty Series by Lisa Bevere, here are some other titles from Charisma House that we think will minister to you…

Out of Control and Loving It!
Lisa Bevere
ISBN: 0-88419-436-1
Retail Price: $12.99

Lisa Bevere's life was a whirlwind of turmoil until she discovered that whenever she was in charge, things ended up in a mess. *Out of Control and Loving It!* is her journey from fearful, frantic control to a haven of rest and peace under God's control.

You Are Not What You Weigh
Lisa Bevere
ISBN: 0-88419-661-5
Retail Price: $10.99

Are you tired of reading trendy diet books, taking faddish pills and ordering the latest in infomercial exercise equipment? This is not another "how-to-lose-weight" book. Dare to believe, and this will be the last book you'll need to finally end your war with food and break free from the bondage of weight watching.

The True Measure of a Woman
Lisa Bevere
ISBN: 0-88419-487-6
Retail Price: $11.99

In her frank, yet gentle manner, Lisa Bevere exposes the subtle influences and blatant lies that hold many women captive. With the unveiling truth of God's Word, she displaces these lies and helps you discover who you are in Christ.

 To pick up a copy of any of these titles, contact your local Christian bookstore or order online at www.charismawarehouse.com.